GOD'S CHURCH

Also by the Author:

God's Promises
God's Son

GOD'S CHURCH

A Book of Stories About the Church
for Young Children

by

DeVere Ramsay

Illustrated by
RITA ENDHOVEN

WILLIAM B. EERDMANS PUBLISHING COMPANY
GRAND RAPIDS, MICHIGAN

Dedicated
to my Mother
who first introduced me to
God's Church

ACKNOWLEDGMENTS

In this third volume I wish to express gratitude to my former teacher, Dr. Ernest Trice Thompson, who for many years was professor of Church History at Union Theological Seminary, Richmond, Virginia. Dr. Thompson read the manuscript and made suggestions for its improvement regarding historical accuracy. I also express my appreciation to Dr. Richard B. Hardie, pastor of the Westover Hills Presbyterian Church, Little Rock, Arkansas, for his permission to tell the story of his World War II experience found here under the title "God's Church Around the World."

Special thanks go to my two sons, John and Mack, who were four and seven years old at the time these stories were told to them, and to their friends, Diane and Arthur Moseley and Stephen Kale, neighbor children who also served as "critics." A word of appreciation is due to Mrs. Davis Yeuell for her help in caring for my children as I typed the manuscript. My husband, Dr. William M. Ramsay, of the Board of Christian Education, Presbyterian Church, U. S., has assisted in the preparation of these stories and I am grateful to him for his help in countless ways. It might even be said that he should be considered a "co-author."

Finally, I am very grateful to the publisher, the editor, and the artist for the fine co-operation they have extended in every way.

—DeVere Ramsay

Richmond, Virginia

Contents

God's Church Is Sent Into the World

(Matthew 28:19-20)

*J*esus *was alive!*

His friends had thought they would never see Him again. But then . . . *Easter came.* Now Jesus was with them — explaining to them all about His life and death. He promised to be with them forever!

Then Jesus told His friends something very important. He told them to go all over the world and tell everyone the Good News. They should tell every man,
every woman,
every boy,
and every girl.

They should tell the whole world about God's love and about God's Son.

This book is the story of some people who have told others about Jesus and showed them God's love. It is about brave men and women who have done what Jesus told them to do. It is the story of people who
taught
and preached
and baptized
and healed
and helped.
It is a book about you, too. For this is the story of
God's Church.

On the Road to Africa
(Acts 8:26-39)

A great man was riding in his chariot along the desert road from Jerusalem to Gaza. He was on his way back to his country, Ethiopia, far away in Africa.

The driver of the chariot cracked his whip to make the horses run. The wheels of the chariot threw hot sand into the air as they rolled along the road. But the tired horses pulled the chariot slower,
and slow-er,
and s-l-o-w-e-r
on the
long, hot trip.

"We must get back to the palace soon!" the Ethiopian man called to the driver. The Ethiopian was an important person in the service of the queen of his country. He had been to Jerusalem to worship in God's House.

As he rode along, the Ethiopian was reading from God's Book. He read from the prophet Isaiah. He read about a kind and good man who was called God's Lamb. But the Ethiopian did not understand.

Suddenly . . .
a man named Philip, one of Jesus' disciples, came running up the road toward the chariot. He heard the Ethiopian reading from God's Book.

"Do you understand what you are reading?" Philip asked.
"How can I, unless someone helps me?" the Ethiopian answered. "Come," he said, "ride with me. Maybe you can tell me what this Book means."

12

13

The driver stopped the chariot.
Philip climbed up and sat down.

"What I do not understand," the Ethiopian said, "is this: Who is the man the prophet is talking about? Is he talking about Moses?"

"No," Philip answered; "he is not talking about Moses."

"Is he talking about himself?"

"No, Isaiah is not talking about himself."

"Is he talking about someone else who lived long ago?"

"No, he is not talking about any of these."

Then Philip told the Good News about Jesus!
He told the Ethiopian that Jesus was God's Son.
He told him that God wants all people to love Jesus.
He told him that God wants all people to be baptized and to belong to His Church.

Just then the chariot came to a stream.

"Look," the Ethiopian said. "Here is water. I would like to be baptized right now!"

So Philip baptized the Ethiopian right there in the desert. Then Philip left him.

But now the Ethiopian sang as he traveled down the road. Now he understood the words that were written in God's Book.

He was happy that he had heard about Jesus.

God's Church was not just for Jews who lived in Palestine.

God's Church was for all people who loved Jesus, of every race and land all over the world. The Ethiopian was happy to be a part of

God's Church

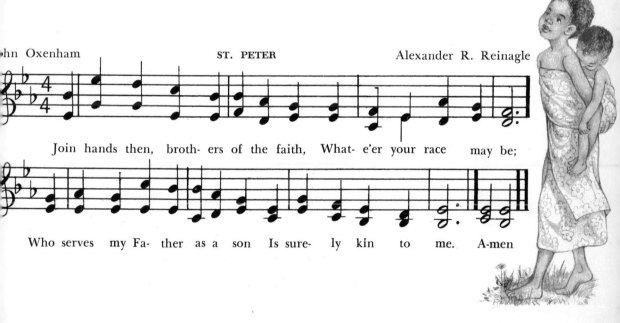

John Oxenham   ST. PETER   Alexander R. Reinagle

Join hands then, broth- ers of the faith, What- e'er your race may be;

Who serves my Fa- ther as a son Is sure- ly kin to me. A-men

15

The Calling of Paul

(Acts 9:1-19)

The Church was having a hard time. People who had not liked Jesus did not like the Church either.

Sometimes soldiers would break up church services.
Sometimes they put church members in jail.
Sometimes they even killed members of God's Church.

One of the men who worked the hardest to stop the Church was Saul of Tarsus. He put many Christians in jail, because he thought that was what God wanted him to do. He went to the priest and said:

"I have worked hard here in Jerusalem to stop people from worshiping Jesus. Let me now go to the city of Damascus and arrest Christians there, too."

So, with his friends, Saul started down the road to Damascus.

But . . .
while he was on the trip
something very
strange happened!

Suddenly . . .
Saul saw a great light.
He covered his eyes.
He fell to the ground.
He heard a voice saying:
"Saul, Saul, why are you doing this to Me?"

"Who are you?" Saul asked.

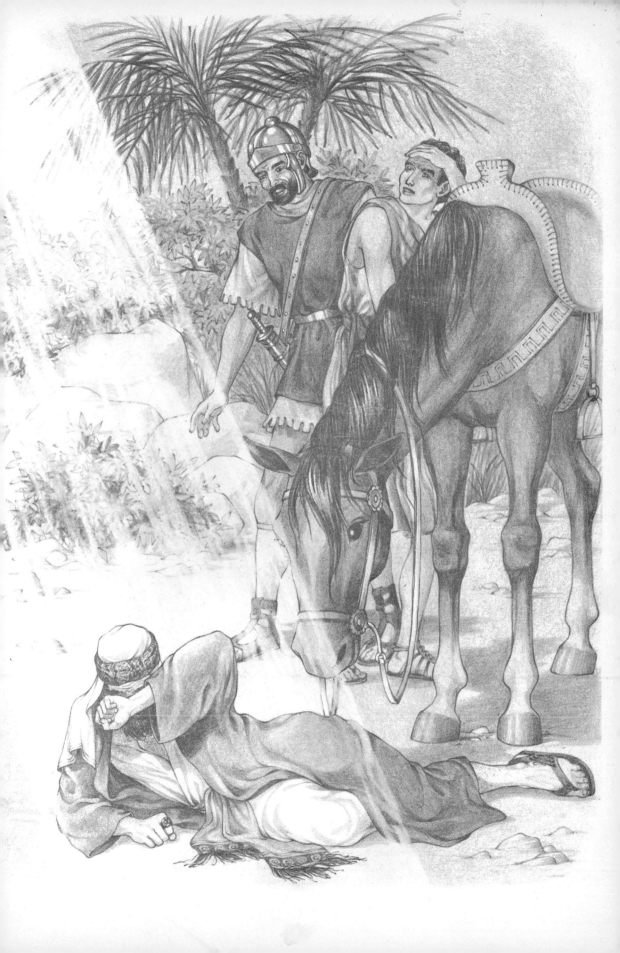

"I am Jesus," said the voice. "Go on to Damascus, and I will tell you what to do when you get there."

When Saul stood up, he discovered that he was blind.

He could not see the sky.
He could not see the road.
He could not see his friends.
They had to lead him by the hand all the way to Damascus.

In Damascus there lived a Christian named Ananias. In a dream God said to him, "Ananias, go to the street called Straight, and there you will find Saul."

Ananias was afraid. He did not want to go, for he had heard of Saul. He said to the Lord, "Go to Saul of Tarsus? But he might put me in jail, as he has so many other Christians!"

But God said, "Yes, Ananias. I want you to go to Saul, and help him see again, for I have chosen this man to tell many people about Jesus. He will be a missionary."

So Ananias did as God told him to do. He went to a certain house on the street called Straight, and there he found Saul.

He did not say to Saul: "You are an unkind man, Saul!" or: "You are a very cruel man, Saul!" Instead, Ananias *touched* Saul, and he called him *Brother Saul!* And at once *Saul could see again!*

Then Ananias baptized Saul. Now Saul, too, was a member of God's Church. From that time on Saul was a very different man. God had changed him. He was so different that he even got a new name. Now people called him Paul.

From then on Paul spent his time telling people about Jesus.

Paul went all over the world building *God's Church.*

A Jailer Hears About Jesus

(Acts 16:19-34)

I t was midnight.

It was dark in the jail at Philippi. The great iron doors were closed and locked. The prisoners were bound to the wall with iron chains. The jailer was asleep.

Some of the prisoners were sleeping.
Some of the prisoners were afraid.
Some of the prisoners were crying.

But two of the prisoners were singing praises to God! Paul and Silas were not afraid. They knew that God would take care of them.

Suddenly. . .

the whole room was shaken.
There was a roar like thunder.
An earthquake broke the big doors open.
And all the chains of the prisoners were broken.

The jailer awoke from his sleep.
Now it was he who was afraid.
"What must I do to be saved?"
he cried.

"Believe in the Lord Jesus, and you will be saved, you and all your family," Paul and Silas answered. Then they told him about Jesus.

The jailer took Paul and Silas and washed their wounds where they had been beaten. *And he and all his family were baptized that very night.*

> The jailer invited Paul and Silas to his home and gave them good food to eat.
> He was happy that he had become a Christian.
> Now even the jailer and his family were a part of *God's Church.*

Beyond Bible Times

Another name for God's people is *God's Church.* Long, long ago, there were not any church *buildings.* So where do you think God's Church met to worship together?

> Sometimes it met in homes.
> Sometimes it met outdoors.
> Sometimes it met beneath the ground in caves. These caves were called catacombs.
> God's Church can meet any time and anywhere.

In Bible times and afterwards it was not always easy to be a Christian. It took brave men and women to be followers of Christ. It took brave boys and girls to be followers of Christ. It takes brave boys and girls today to be followers of Christ.

The early Christians often had to hide when they came together to worship Jesus. Then God's Church met in secret.

Doors were locked.

Prayers were said in whispers.

Someone stood guard to let the Christians know when people came who might take them away to prison.

And some Christians *were* arrested.

Some Christians even had to die for their faith!

But whatever happened, the Christians knew that God loved them, for *nothing can separate the Christian from the love of Christ!*

God's Church began to spread over the whole world. From

Palestine

to Africa

to Rome

across Europe

men and women, boys and girls in every part of the known world began to hear . . . and to tell the Good News about Jesus.

Missionaries in Bible times, and then others who followed them in later years, took the gospel message all over the world. These missionaries helped others to become members of *God's Church.*

Patrick and the Pirates

(St. Patrick, A.D. 389-461)

Pirates had come from the sea to the coast of Britain.
They were robbers who sailed in big ships.
Everywhere they went they stole what they could.
Sometimes the pirates took sheep.
Sometimes the pirates took gold.
Sometimes the pirates took silver.
And sometimes the pirates took with them
little boys.

Patrick was a boy who lived on the coast of Britain.
His father was a deacon in the church.
His grandfather was an elder in the church.
But Patrick told later on that he himself was
not a very good boy in those days.

When the pirates came to Britain and saw young Patrick, they made the boy go with them.

They sailed across the sea to the land of Ireland. They sold him to a farmer to be a slave. Patrick spent his time taking care of the farmer's sheep.

As Patrick took care of the sheep, he began to think. He began to remember some of the things his father and grandfather had taught him about God.

He remembered Bible stories they had told him.

He may have remembered David, who had been a shepherd boy, too.

And we know he remembered Jesus, who told a story about a little lost sheep.

Patrick began to pray.
Sometimes he would talk to God a hundred times in one
    day. *God heard Patrick's prayer.*

One day Patrick learned that a ship was waiting in the
harbor, many miles away. "Perhaps that ship will take me
home!" thought Patrick.

And so,
one night,
while the farmer was asleep,
young Patrick slipped away.
He was very quiet.
He walked on tiptoe.
He did not say a word.
        He walked for miles
and miles and miles.

At last he came to the harbor where the ship was waiting.
Patrick asked the captain to let him work on the ship.

He sailed many weeks. He had many adventures on land
and on sea. One day Patrick landed on the coast of Britain.
And at last he was home once more. He must have hoped that
he would never have to leave home again.

But . . .
        one night Patrick had a dream.
        He saw a postman carrying letters.
        One of those letters was for Patrick.
        Patrick read the first words of the letter.
It began: "The voice of the Irish . . . ."

Then, in his dream, Patrick heard voices of people in
Ireland. The voices said, "Return, holy boy, and walk with
us once more!"

When Patrick woke up, he knew that God was calling him to go back to Ireland. He must tell the people there about Jesus.

Patrick did not want to go. But God had called him, and he had to obey.

First he went to school.
He studied his Bible.
He learned to be a missionary.
At last he sailed away to the land of the Irish again.

All over Ireland Patrick told the people about Jesus and about God's love for them.

Before Patrick began to preach in Ireland, almost no one in that land had heard of Jesus. But while Patrick lived and worked there, nearly all the Irish people became Christians.

Every year, on St. Patrick's Day, Irish people everywhere remember this great missionary.

On that day
songs are sung,
music is made,
parades are held,
as people thank God for Patrick, who did so much in the building of
God's Church.

The Little Brother of the Poor

(St. Francis of Assisi, 1182-1226)

Many years ago there lived in Italy a young man whose name was Francis. Francis was a soldier.

One day, when he was home from the wars, he went to a little church to pray. The church was so old that it was falling down. There were many holes in the roof and the walls. As Francis was praying, he seemed to hear Jesus saying to him:
"Do you see how My House is in ruins?"

Francis thought that the voice was speaking of the little old church, and so he decided that he would fix it.

His first idea as to how to build God's House was not a very good one. He took some cloth from his father's store and sold it to get money to fix the church. When his father found out about it, he did not like it, for it was not Francis' cloth to sell.

Then Francis decided to try something else. He went from house to house, asking for bricks and stones and hammers and saws with which to repair the church. With the help from some friends, the little old church was rebuilt. After that Francis repaired another church
and another
and another.

But this was not quite the way God meant it when He told Francis to build His Church.

One day Francis was walking along the road. He saw a sick man who was begging. Francis gave the man some money and walked on. Then something made him turn and go back to the sick man. He knelt down beside the beggar,

put his arms around him,
and said, "I love you!"

This was the way God wanted him to build the Church.

Soon Francis gathered more and more friends. They called
themselves "Brothers of the Poor."

When someone was sick,
    he could come to the "Brothers of the Poor," and they
    would help him.
When someone was hungry,
    he could come to the "Brothers of the Poor," and they
    would help him.

When someone was lonely,
  he could come to the "Brothers of the Poor," and they
  would help him.

The "Brothers of the Poor" showed people God's love by
what they did for others.

Francis loved everything God had made:
  He loved poor people.
  He loved rich people.
  He loved the birds.
  He loved the animals.

In old books it is written that Francis loved everything
God made so much that he even used to talk to the birds and
animals about the love of God.

  It was by *loving* that Francis really built
  God's Church.

God's Church and God's Word

(Martin Luther, 1483-1546)

Sometimes the Church does wrong things.
  Sometimes church members forget about the Bible.
  Sometimes they think that they can buy God's love.
  Sometimes they forget that Jesus alone is the Head of
    the Church.

Then God has to make His Church right again. Making
the Church right again is called *Reformation*. Once it
happened like this:

It was Halloween. A group of people were on their way to the church at Wittenberg, in Germany, to pray. One of them, Martin Luther, stopped at the door. He had a hammer and a piece of paper in his hands.

"Bang, bang, bang!" went his hammer. Martin Luther was nailing the piece of paper to the church door. On that paper was written a long list of things — ninety-five things — that Martin Luther felt the Church was forgetting about God. He felt that the Church in his day was doing things, and teaching things, that were not found in the Bible. Martin Luther had come to understand that God tells us in His Book, the Bible, what He wants His Church to do.

Soon Martin began to preach what the Bible says:
He preached to men and women.
He preached to boys and girls.
He preached to poor people.
He preached to rich people.
He preached all over the country . . .
and the king did not like it.

"You must take back these words," the king said. "You must say only what I tell you to say."

"No," replied Luther, "I must say what God tells me in the Bible. Here I stand. I can do nothing else."

When Martin Luther had said that, his friends told him, "You must hide from the king."
They took him to a castle far away.
They dressed him in different clothes.
"Now the king's men will not know you, if they should see you," Martin's friends said.

Hidden in the castle, Martin Luther spent his time writing the Bible in the language of the people. Before that, there

were only Bibles in a strange language they could not read.

When at last he could come out of hiding, he began to preach from the Bible again. Soon his friends were taking Bibles all over Germany. They took Bibles to Switzerland. They took Bibles to France. They took Bibles to Holland. They took Bibles to England.

And there is a Bible in your home today, partly because of Martin Luther and other men like him, long ago. Those men of the Reformation reminded God's people that the Bible is the Book that tells us what we must do as members of

God's Church

God's Church in a New Land
(The Pilgrims and Thanksgiving, 1620, 1621)

The King of England was putting many Christians in jail. He did not like the way they wanted to worship God.

"You must go to my church, and you must worship just as I tell you," he said.

But these Christians had read their Bibles. They wanted to worship the way they believed God told them in His Word.
They wanted to sing their own hymns.
They wanted to obey Jesus' words.
They wanted to pray in their own way.
But the king would not let them.
He wanted them to go to his church.

Then . . . they heard of a strange new land, far away, a land called America.

"Let us go to America," said one of these Christians. "There we will be free to worship in *God's Church* the way we believe God wants us to worship Him."

So, one day, a group of these people, who were called Pilgrims, got on a ship, *The Mayflower*, and began the dangerous voyage across the ocean. They sailed many days.
They sailed many nights.
Often they were hungry,
and thirsty,
and cold.

Weeks went by.
Months went by . . .
until at last they saw
in the distance
the coast of
America.

37

The ship landed.
The Pilgrims went ashore.

They bowed their heads and
gave thanks to God
that He had brought them safely to the new land.

There was work to be done.
With axes and saws the Pilgrims cut down trees.
They cleared the land.
They planted seeds.
They built homes.
And they built a church.

That first winter was very hard for the Pilgrims in the
new country. But when spring came,
the seeds began to grow.
Friendly Indians taught them to hunt and fish.
There was food for everyone now.
God was taking care of the Pilgrims.

When harvest time came in the fall, the Pilgrims had a
special day on which they gave thanks to God.

They invited the friendly Indians to come.
They played games together.
They had a big dinner of turkey and cranberries
and pumpkins and corn and beans.
And they all gave thanks to God.

This was one of the first Thanksgiving Days in America.

Every year on Thanksgiving Day we thank God in our homes and in

God's Church.

God's Church Around the World

(Naha and the Sailor)

Dick lived in Texas.

Some people in Texas wore cowboy hats.
Some people wore cowboy boots.

But when the Second World War began,
Dick put on a sailor suit.

Later the Navy put Dick in
command of a ship that sailed across the South Pacific Ocean.

Near the end of the war, Dick was ordered to take his ship to a certain island to see how things were there.

The ship stopped close to the shore.
The sailors got off and began to wade toward the beach.
They did not know what they would find on the island.
Some of the sailors were afraid, for there was a war on, and anything could happen.

Suddenly . . .

they heard shouts and screams.
People were rushing upon them.
The sailors thought they were enemies.

Then they began to laugh. The people coming toward them were little boys and girls! They were shouting the only English words they knew — *candy* and *chew gum*. The sailors now knew that Americans had been here before.

Dick sent some of his men back to the ship to get candy and chewing gum. Soon the sailors were giving each child a candy bar and a package of gum. In a few minutes the children ran back to their village, laughing and happy.

Dick started to walk toward the village, too. But now he felt something pulling at his pants leg. He looked down.

There was a little girl. She held up a chocolate-covered hand and said, "Candy?" Dick was sure she must already have had a candy bar, but he smiled, and gave her another one. Then he went on.

A little later he felt somebody pulling at his other pants leg. He looked down, and there was the same little girl. "Chew gum?" she said.

Dick knew she had already had her chewing gum, so he picked her up, put her on his shoulder, and began to carry her toward the village.

There was not much Dick and the little girl could say to each other, because they could not understand each other's language. "But perhaps we can learn each other's name," he thought. So he pointed to himself and said, "Dick! Dick!" The little girl seemed to know what he meant. She pointed to herself and said, "Naha!"

But that was all they could say. Then Dick started to hum a song. Suddenly little Naha started to hum along the same tune. Then she began to sing the words. She sang them in her language, and Dick sang the words in his language. They both knew the same song!

I am sure you know it too.

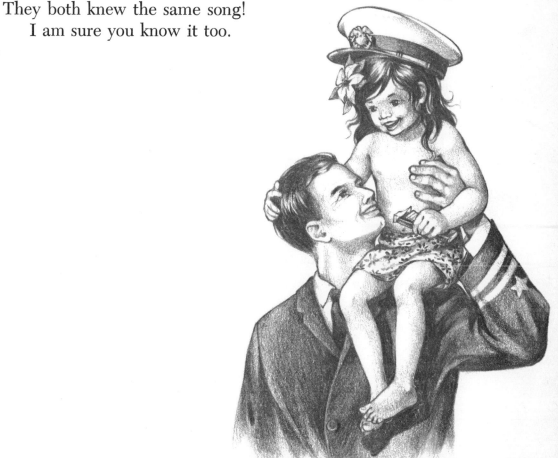

It goes like this:

Anna B. Warner   William B. Bradbury

Je- sus loves me! This I know, For the Bi- ble tells me so.

Lit- tle ones to Him be- long; They are weak, but He is strong. Yes, Je- sus

loves me! Yes, Je- sus loves me! Yes, Je- sus loves me! The Bi- ble tells me so.

Now Dick knew he had nothing to fear on the island. God's Church had come here. Just as he had a little sister in Texas, so he now had brothers and sisters on the island.

The people were of a different race. Their skin was a different color. They spoke a different language. But still they were his brothers and sisters. They were members with him in

God's Church.

44

God's Church and You

(The First Sunday School, 1780)

Robert Raikes was a newspaperman in Gloucester, England. He wrote about many things in his newspaper. One day a lady said to him, "Sir, you should see our streets on Sunday. They are filled with little boys and girls who have nothing to do. They are poor and dirty and cold and hungry. But, worst of all, nobody teaches them anything!"

What the lady told him made Robert Raikes think. Finally he got an idea. "The boys and girls in our town need a chance to learn," he said to himself. "They need to learn to read,

and to write;

and they need to know about God.

I will start a school that will meet every Sunday."

Robert Raikes hired four teachers. He promised to pay them fourteen pennies a day. "Go into the streets and invite every boy and girl to come to our school," he told them.

He gave each teacher a spelling book and a Bible.

"Teach all the boys and girls to read and to write. And above all, teach them to know the love of the Lord Jesus."

Many boys and girls came. They were so glad that they could learn about Jesus. Every Sunday they studied for six hours in the school that was started by kind Mr. Raikes. His school was the very first *Sunday school* in all the world.

But soon there were more Sunday schools.
There were Sunday schools in London.
There were Sunday schools in Toronto.
There were Sunday schools in New York.
. . . And now there are Sunday schools in your home town.
One day you became a pupil in
Sunday school, too, for *you* are a part of
God's Church.

ABOUT THE AUTHOR

DeVere Maxwell Ramsay, a native of Tuscaloosa, Alabama, is a graduate of the University of Alabama and has a M.A. degree in Bible from the Presbyterian School of Christian Education. Before her marriage she served as a director of Christian education in South Carolina and in Alabama. In recent years Mrs. Ramsay has been a teacher of nursery church school leaders and is a children's work consultant for the new Covenant Life Curriculum sponsored by the Presbyterian Church, U.S., and the Reformed Church in America.

The author is married to Dr. William M. Ramsay, director of adult education with the Board of Christian Education, Presbyterian Church, U.S. Their home is in Richmond, Virginia. Dr. Ramsay is also an author and has published several books. Together Dr. and Mrs. Ramsay have written church school curriculum materials for children and youth. The Ramsays have two young sons, Mack and John.

ABOUT THE ARTIST

Rita Endhoven was born in The Netherlands. When she was six years old her family emigrated to Canada, where her father is principal of a Christian day school in Fort William, Ontario. Her mother taught school in The Netherlands, and Miss Endhoven, too, is now a schoolteacher.

The artist's talent is wholly natural, and runs in the family. Her mother and a younger sister are equally gifted. **God's Church** is the third book Miss Endhoven has illustrated, and in doing it she again worked closely with the author, as she did when illustrating the first books in the series, **God's Promises** and **God's Son**. In the future Miss Endhoven hopes to specialize in the study of art.

48